W9-ACB-537

Living in
Suburban
Communities

by Kristin Sterling

first step nonfiction

Lerner Publications Company · Minneapolis

Welcome to my **community.**

A community is a place where people feel at home.

3

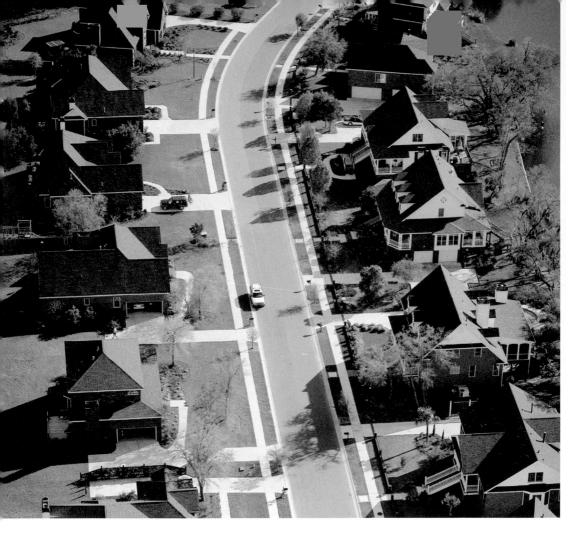

I live in a **suburban** community.

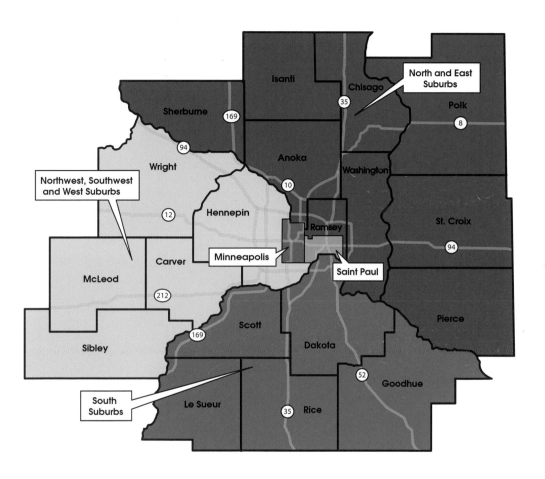

North and East
Suburbs

Isanti

Chisago

35

Polk

8

Sherburne

169

94

Wright

Anoka

Washington

Northwest, Southwest
and West Suburbs

12

Hennepin

10

Ramsey

St. Croix

94

Minneapolis

Carver

Saint Paul

McLeod

Pierce

212

Scott

169

Dakota

Sibley

52

Goodhue

South
Suburbs

Le Sueur

35 Rice

Suburban communities are also called suburbs.

Suburbs are between the city and the country.

Most suburbs were once
grasslands, farms, or forests.

There are many things to
see in a suburb.

Let's take a look around!

I see **neighborhoods** full of houses.

I see yards with swing sets and gardens.

I see people in cars,
buses, and trains.

They are going into the city
to work.

I see children playing
in parks.

I see families shopping
at stores.

Suburbs are **convenient** and roomy.

Do you live in a suburb?

Where are suburbs?

city

suburbs

country

Suburbs

Have you ever seen a dartboard? There is a big spot in the middle called the bull's-eye. There are rings around the bull's-eye. A city is like a bull's-eye. Suburbs are like the rings around a bull's-eye. Suburbs are built around the edges of a city. They provide housing for people who work in the city. Many suburban people like living between the city and the country.

Suburban Facts

 Mesa, Arizona, is the biggest suburb in America. It is bigger than many cities!

 When cars were invented, people began to drive to work. They could move farther away from their workplaces. This led to the growth of suburbs.

 Some people who live in the suburbs ride buses, subways, or trains to work in the city.

 Some suburbs have neighborhoods where all of the houses look the same.

 Levittown, New York, is one of the most famous suburbs in the world. It was built for soldiers and their families when they returned from World War II.

 Suburban communities are sometimes nicknamed "the 'burbs."

Glossary

 community – a place where people live together and feel at home.

 convenient – easy to use, comfortable

 neighborhoods – groups of homes

 suburban – of or like a suburb. A suburb is a community built near a city.

Index

The photographs in this book are used with the permission of: © Mike Powell/The Image Bank/Getty Images, cover; © John Kelly/The Image Bank/Getty Images, pp. 2, 9, 22 (top); © age fotostock/SuperStock, p. 3; © Jason Hawkes/CORBIS, p. 4; © David Hanson/Stone/Getty Images, p. 6; © Philip Gould/CORBIS, p. 7; © Ariel Skelley/Riser/Getty Images, p. 8; © Skyscan/CORBIS, pp. 10, 22 (second from bottom); © DCA Productions/Taxi/Getty Images, p. 11; © PhotoDisc Royalty Free by Getty Images, p. 12; © Kim Karpeles/Alamy, p. 13; © Darren Robb/The Image Bank/Getty Images, p. 14; © J. Silver/SuperStock, p. 15; © Nick Daly/Photonica/Getty Images, pp. 16, 22 (second from top); © Ariel Skelley/CORBIS, p. 17.

Map on pages 5 and 22 (bottom) by © Bill Hauser/Independent Picture Service.
Illustration on page 18 by © Bill Hauser/Independent Picture Service.

Lerner Publications Company
A division of Lerner Publishing Group, Inc.
241 First Avenue North
Minneapolis, MN 55401 U.S.A.

Website address: www.lernerbooks.com

Library of Congress Cataloging-in-Publication Data

Sterling, Kristin.
    Living in suburban communities / by Kristin Sterling.
        p.   cm. — (First step nonfiction—communities)
    Includes index.
    ISBN13: 978–0–8225–8598–5 (lib. bdg. : alk. paper)
    1. Suburban life—Juvenile literature. 2. Community life—Juvenile literature.
3. Communities—Juvenile literature. I. Title.
HT351.S84 2008
307.74—dc22   2007006363

Manufactured in the United States of America
1 2 3 4 5 6 – DP – 13 12 11 10 09 08